The Raven Steals the Light

ETNG

THE RAVEN
STEALS THE LIGHT

Native American Tales

Bill Reid and Robert Bringhurst
Foreword by Claude Levi-Strauss

SHAMBHALA
Boston
1996

Shambhala Publications, Inc.
Horticultural Hall
300 Massachusetts Avenue
Boston, Massachusetts 02115

© 1984 by Bill Reid and Robert Bringhurst
Drawings © 1984 by Bill Reid
Foreword © 1995 by Claude Lévi-Strauss
Published by arrangement with Douglas & McIntyre

All rights reserved. No part of this book may be
reproduced in any form or by any means, electronic or
mechanical, including photocopying, recording, or by any
information storage and retrieval system, without
permission in writing from the publisher.

9 8 7 6 5 4 3 2 1

First Shambhala Edition
Printed in Canada
⊗ This edition is printed on acid-free paper that meets the
American National Standards Institute Z39.48 Standard.
Distributed in the United States by Random House, Inc.

See page 154 for Library of Congress
Cataloguing-in-Publication data.

Contents

Foreword

In the summer of 1974, my wife, our young son, and I were traveling through British Columbia in what is called in that country a camper. One evening, on the coast of Vancouver Island, we were waiting for the ferry that was to take us and our vehicle, which was also our home, to Alert Bay, a very small island in the Strait of Georgia that is inhabited by Kwakiutl Indians, who consider it a sanctuary.

Night was falling, and there was still no ferry. Its lights were visible in the distance; it seemed to be engaged in a complicated maneuver. We learned that it had been called to another island because of a medical emergency and that we would have to wait several hours.

The few of us on the wooden dock had no choice but to put up with the delay. A young Indian-looking man wearing a pink track suit started a conversation. He told me he was a champion of some sport or other (I don't remember which). Kwakiutl by birth, he had always lived far from his family and was going home to become a sculptor—a good trade, he explained, in which one didn't pay taxes. He added that it would be difficult; he would have to start by learning his language, which he had never spoken.

His words seemed very revealing, since the traditional arts of the Indians of the Northwest Coast are indissolubly linked to legends and myths. No other art has broken through the barrier between the natural and the supernatural worlds with such momentum. Over the millennia, the Indians of the Northwest Coast have developed graphic and sculptural conventions and employed stylistic devices in which human and nonhuman traits are combined, interwoven, and transmuted. They give life to a reality hitherto unimaginable, one to which the viewer is immediately drawn. This reality consists of beings of a third type: neither human nor animal, but both at once. As the poet says, these beings cast upon us a familiar eye, and they take us back to the time evoked by this book, when animals could assume human form and knew the manners and the language of humans perfectly well.

These beings all played a determining role

in the history of the people, or rather of the clans, the houses, the families. The way in which the artist conjoins them or represents their particular traits evokes, in detail, the moment at which they appeared. They are great ancestors, protectors, and sometimes formidable adversaries that humans met in very ancient times. The circumstances of those meetings, as described in the myths and legends, explain the social distinctions, the hierarchy, and the rituals. They alone allow us to understand the form and decoration of the masks and emblems worn at ceremonies.

Whether they be of Haida origin, like Bill Reid, or Tlingit, Tsimshian, Kwakiutl, or Bella Coola, Northwest Coast artists must also be scholars. They must incorporate into their work the most subtle local nuances of a knowledge that, in many respects, constitutes the common heritage of all those peoples. Over the centuries, they traded with each other, fought each other, intermarried, and took prisoners who became slaves. Whether hostile or peaceful, the incessant contact between them drew the styles of painting and sculpture, as well as the myths, closer together. They turned the coastal cultures into a veritable civilization.

The first myth in this collection provides a good example of major cosmological themes that are common to all the peoples in the region. It involves the Raven, a deity of the type called in English a trickster, which the old French word *décepteur* matches to perfection. The fact that the Amerindians placed a deceitful, insolent, libidinous, and often grotesque character with a penchant for scatology in the forefront of their pantheon sometimes surprises people. But indigenous thought places the Raven at the turning point between two eras. In the beginning, nothing was impossible; the most extravagant wishes could come true. However, the present era, in which humans and animals have acquired distinct natures, is stamped with the seal of necessity. In the world inhabited by man, social life obeys rules, and nature dictates its will. We can no longer do just anything. The Trickster discovers this, often at his own expense. And because his immoderate appetites make him the foremost victim of these nascent constraints, it is up to him to make them definitive and to establish their terms. In a universe that is undergoing constant change, the Raven is both the ultimate rebel and the foremost maker of laws.

One of Bill Reid's masterworks, which has never been brought to Paris for exhibition because of its size, represents the Raven's discovery of the first humans, related in one of the myths in this collection. The sculptor depicted the Raven as a majestic but shady character, which shows how fully the sculptor must allow himself to be permeated by the substance of the myths. Bill Reid displays his intimate knowledge of the myths in two ways: through extremely refined illustrations and through his stories. To be sure, his versions cannot claim the density or the complexity of the long versions collected (almost all in the original Haida) and published by John Swanton at the beginning of the century. But these already had lacunae, and perhaps there were other versions, still richer in detail, that we shall never know.

Bill Reid modestly refers to his stories as "mere glancing versions of the grand old tales," but they are nevertheless very accurate. In the word-for-word translations that have been published in scholarly works, no care was taken to preserve the charm of these marvellous stories. The fruit of an inspired collaboration between an artist and a poet, this book makes us more sensitive to their power of seduction, their charm, and their freshness.

CLAUDE LÉVI-STRAUSS

Preface

I consider myself one of the most fortunate of men, to have lived at a time when some of the old Haidas and their peers among the Northwest Coast peoples were still alive, and to have had the privilege of knowing them.

Protected by the sure conviction of who they were, they survived terrible assaults on the way of life which had served them so well for so long, and they responded to the rigours of an arrogant, often unfriendly, disdainful world with dignity and courtesy, embodied in inbred instinct for doing the right thing. I certainly shall not see their like again in my time.

I would like to dedicate this little book to one of these men, Henry Young of Skidegate, who was my friend when I was twenty and he was in his eighties. I wish I had had more patience and had spent the tiny part of my life he requested, to learn something of the wonderful language he spoke so resonantly and well, and to learn more of the stories of all the myth-creatures whose many adventures instructed, informed and entertained the Haidas during their long history.

Henry was the repository of much of the myth and legend of the Southern Haidas, trained as a boy to carry on a long bardic tradition. If I had listened longer and more carefully, we might now be able to tell you the true stories of the Raven and all his fellows, instead of these slight entertainments, mere glancing versions of the grand old tales.

As entertainments, I hope they amuse, even inform. But let us begin with a request for indulgence from all the great storytellers of the past, whom we salute in the person of Gyitadzlius, Henry Young.

BILL REID
Vancouver, 1984

A Note to the Reader

Haida Gwaii, the Islands of the People, lie equidistant from Luxor, Machu Picchu, Ninevah and Timbuktu. On the white man's maps, where every islet and scrap of land, inhabited or otherwise, sits now in the shadow of somebody's national flag, and is named for preference after a monarch or a politician, Haida Gwaii are shown as the westernmost extremity of Canada, and they are named not for the Haida, who have always lived there, nor for the Raven, who somewhat inadvertently put them there, but for a woman who never saw them. Her name was Sophie Charlotte von Mecklenburg-Strelitz, but the British called her simply Queen Charlotte, for she was the wife of the Mad King of England, George III.

So the Raven, who often likes to call a rose a skunk cabbage, just to see what trouble he can cause, has tricked us again, Haidas and whites alike, with this one. He has us trained now to point to Haida Gwaii and say "Queen Charlotte Islands."

These stories were told there well before Queen Charlotte's time.

The Raven Steals the Light

The Raven Steals the Light

Before there was anything, before the great flood had covered the earth and receded, before the animals walked the earth or the trees covered the land or the birds flew between the trees, even before the fish and the whales and seals swam in the sea, an old man lived in a house on the bank of a river with his only child, a daughter. Whether she was as beautiful as hemlock fronds against the spring sky at sunrise or as ugly as a sea slug doesn't really matter very much to this story, which takes place mainly in the dark.

Because at that time the whole world was dark. Inky, pitchy, all-consuming dark, blacker than a thousand stormy winter midnights, blacker than anything anywhere has been since.

The reason for all this blackness has to do with the old man in the house by the river, who had a box which contained a box which contained a box which contained an infinite number of boxes each nestled in a box slightly larger than itself until finally there was a box so small all it could contain was all the light in the universe.

The Raven, who of course existed at that time, because he had always existed and always would, was somewhat less than satisfied with this state of affairs, since it led to an awful lot of blundering around and bumping into things. It slowed him down a good deal in his pursuit of food and other fleshly pleasures, and in his constant effort to interfere and to change things.

Eventually, his bumbling around in the dark took him close to the home of the old man. He first heard a little singsong voice muttering away. When he followed the voice, he soon came to the wall of the house, and there, placing his ear against the planking, he could just make out the words, "I have a box and inside the box is another box and inside it are many more boxes, and in the smallest box of all is all the light in the world, and it is all mine and I'll never give any of it to anyone, not even to my daughter, because, who knows, she may be as homely as a sea slug, and neither she nor I would like to know that."

It took only an instant for the Raven to decide to steal the light for himself, but it took a lot longer for him to invent a way to do so.

First he had to find a door into the house. But no matter how many times he circled it or how carefully he felt the planking, it remained a smooth, unbroken barrier. Sometimes he heard either the old man or his daughter leave the house to get water or for some other reason, but they always departed from the side of the house opposite to him, and when he ran around to the other side the wall seemed as unbroken as ever.

Finally, the Raven retired a little way upstream and thought and thought about how he could enter the house. As he did so, he began to think more and more of the young girl who lived there, and thinking of her began to stir more than just the Raven's imagination.

"It's probable that she's as homely as a sea slug," he said to himself, "but on the other hand, she may be as beautiful as the fronds of the hemlock would be against a bright spring sunrise, if only there were light enough to make one." And in that idle speculation, he found the solution to his problem.

He waited until the young woman, whose footsteps he could distinguish by now from those of her father, came to the river to gather water. Then he changed himself into a single hemlock needle, dropped himself into the river and floated down just in time to be caught in the basket which the girl was dipping in the river.

Even in his much diminished form, the Raven was able to make at least a very small magic—enough to make the girl so thirsty she took a deep drink from the basket, and in doing so, swallowed the needle.

The Raven slithered down deep into her warm insides and found a soft, comfortable spot, where he transformed himself once more, this time into a very small human being, and went to sleep for a long while. And as he slept he grew.

The young girl didn't have any idea what was happening to her, and of course she didn't tell her father, who noticed nothing unusual because it was so dark—until suddenly he became very aware indeed of a new presence in the house, as the Raven at last emerged triumphantly in the shape of a human boychild.

He was—or would have been, if anyone could have seen him—a strange-looking boy, with a long, beaklike nose and a few feathers here and there. In addition, he had the shining eyes of the Raven, which would have given his face a bright, inquisitive appearance—if anyone could have seen these features then.

And he was noisy. He had a cry that contained all the noises of a spoiled child and an angry raven—yet he could sometimes speak as softly as the wind in the hemlock boughs, with an echo of that beautiful other sound, like an organic bell, which is also part of every raven's speech.

At times like that his grandfather grew to love this strange new member of his household and spent many hours playing with him, making him toys and inventing games for him.

As he gained more and more of the affection and confidence of the old man, the Raven felt more intently around the house, trying to find where the light was hidden. After much exploration, he was convinced it was kept in the big box which stood in the corner of the house. One day he cautiously lifted the lid, but of course could see nothing, and all he could feel was another box. His grandfather, however, heard his precious treasure chest being disturbed, and he dealt very harshly with the would-be thief, threatening dire punishment if the Ravenchild ever touched the box again.

This triggered a tidal wave of noisy protests, followed by tender importuning, in which the Raven never mentioned the light, but only pleaded for the largest box. That box, said the Ravenchild, was the one thing he needed to make him completely happy.

As most if not all grandfathers have done

since the beginning, the old man finally yielded and gave his grandchild the outermost box. This contented the boy for a short time—but as most if not all grandchildren have done since the beginning, the Raven soon demanded the next box.

It took many days and much cajoling, carefully balanced with well-planned tantrums, but one by one the boxes were removed. When only a few were left, a strange radiance, never before seen, began to infuse the darkness of the house, disclosing vague shapes and their shadows, still too dim to have definite form. The Ravenchild then begged in his most pitiful voice to be allowed to hold the light for just a moment.

His request was instantly refused, but of course in time his grandfather yielded. The old man lifted the light, in the form of a beautiful, incandescent ball, from the final box and tossed it to his grandson.

He had only a glimpse of the child on whom he had lavished such love and affection, for even as the light was travelling toward him, the child changed from his human form to a huge, shining black shadow, wings spread and beak open, waiting. The Raven snapped up the light in his jaws, thrust his great wings downward and shot through the smokehole of the house into the huge darkness of the world.

That world was at once transformed. Mountains and valleys were starkly silhouetted, the river sparkled with broken reflections, and everywhere life began to stir. And from far away, another great winged shape launched itself into the air, as light struck the eyes of the Eagle for the first time and showed him his target.

The Raven flew on, rejoicing in his wonderful new possession, admiring the effect it had on the world below, revelling in the experience of being able to see where he was going, instead of flying blind and hoping for the best. He was having such a good time that he never saw the Eagle until the Eagle was almost upon him. In a panic he swerved to escape the savage outstretched claws, and in doing so he dropped a good half of the light he was carrying. It fell to the rocky ground below and there broke into pieces—one large piece and too many small ones to count. They bounced back into the sky and remain there even today as the moon and the stars that glorify the night.

The Eagle pursued the Raven beyond the

rim of the world, and there, exhausted by the long chase, the Raven finally let go of his last piece of light. Out beyond the rim of the world, it floated gently on the clouds and started up over the mountains lying to the east.

Its first rays caught the smokehole of the house by the river, where the old man sat weeping bitterly over the loss of his precious light and the treachery of his grandchild. But as the light reached in, he looked up and for the first time saw his daughter, who had been quietly sitting during all this time, completely bewildered by the rush of events.

The old man saw that she was as beautiful as the fronds of a hemlock against a spring sky at sunrise, and he began to feel a little better.

The Raven Steals the Salmon
from the Beaver House

The Raven had grown tired of Haida Gwaii and had flown to the mainland, where he had heard there were lakes and streams—things not then to be found in the Islands. The lakes and streams as such didn't interest him very much, but the thought of the tasty fish he might find in them certainly did.

He landed on a beach and was walking along feeling hungry and alone when, coming around a low headland, he met two men whom he knew to be beavers. They were very friendly, and they saw at once that the Raven was in great need of something to eat and a warm place to rest his wings. They fed him the little they had with them—and it was real food, not alder bark, such as beavers eat most of the time. No ordinary human beings such as we know them now were yet to be found on the earth. The Raven hadn't got round to creating them. But the two beavers, since they had decided to visit the beach, were in the midst of a human transformation, and so, to the Raven's delight, they not only looked like humans but were eating a rich and varied diet, just as humans like to do.

They invited him to come to their house, and the Raven gladly consented. The house wasn't far away, and when they arrived the

Raven saw it was a great place indeed, a great beam-and-plank edifice with a magnificent pole in front of it. As they entered, the Raven saw a wonderfully painted screen which stretched across the rear of the house, and he seemed to hear the rush of powerful rivers and the tinkle of pleasant streams from behind the screen. Most exciting of all, he seemed to hear a sound which could only be that of a good-sized fish jumping.

The Raven asked about the sounds, as he could not recall having seen any bodies of water around the house before he came in. But the men, who were really beavers, said they could hear nothing.

One of them soon started a fire in the firepit in the center of the house. The other stepped through an opening in the screen, which shimmered most strangely in the firelight, and he came back shortly carrying two spring salmon. The two men cooked these on the fire and offered a portion to the Raven. All three had a satisfying meal and then went to sleep.

Next morning the same thing happened— one man lighting the fire, the other getting the fish from behind the screen, and all three eating until they could eat no more.

The Raven stayed in the beavers' house for many days, enjoying the food and also the company of his hosts. But one morning he woke to find that the men, who he'd known all along were beavers, had reassumed their beaver shape. Instead of the pleasant sounds of his companions preparing the morning meal, he heard only the grunts and heaves of the beavers as they cut down trees and hauled them to the lodge. And much worse, instead of succulent salmon, he was served a stick of very tough wood for his breakfast. The Raven grew suddenly homesick for his native islands and decided it was time to return.

But he certainly wasn't going home without trying to find the secret that lay behind the screen, so as soon as the beavers went out again on a tree-cutting expedition, the Raven went to the rear of the house and looked everywhere for the opening. He had no success until he remembered how one of the beavers had built up the fire before the other had penetrated the screen. He too built a fire, and when he had done that the screen seemed to dissolve like coastal mist before him. He walked right through the insubstantial images which had been solid wood before, and found himself looking out over a vast expanse of land dotted and traced with lakes and rivers, all of them full of fish and all of the fish making their way to their home waters to spawn and die.

The Raven in his excitement tried to pick up as many fish as possible to take home with him, but trying as he did to hold so many at a time, he kept on dropping all of them.

He sat down and thought about what he could do. "It's nice country," he said, "but it's sort of flat, not like the Islands. I wonder what would happen if I lifted the corner of it here and tried to roll it into something I could handle." So the Raven pulled at the ground near his feet, and he found it came loose from the bedrock quite easily. He started rolling it up like a cedarbark blanket, and after a short time he had all the lakes and rivers and streams in a neat, convenient roll, which he took in his strong beak. Then he flew rapidly back through the screen and headed for the Islands.

Before he arrived, a lot of the water from the rolled-up rivers had drained away, but many of the streams and the little lakes remained. And most importantly, the fish were safe.

When he reached the Islands at last, the Raven was tired from carrying his load, and he was happy to drop the roll and let what remained of the lakes and streams fall where they might. That's why today nearly every one of the Haida Islands is spattered with little lakes and small but very rich streams—the refuge each year for millions of spawning salmon, some of which still provide welcome meals for the Raven and all his relations.

The Raven and the First Men

The great flood which had covered the earth for so long had at last receded, and even the thin strip of sand now called Rose Spit, stretching north from Naikun village, lay dry. The Raven had flown there to gorge himself on the delicacies left by the receding water, so for once he wasn't hungry. But his other appetites—lust, curiosity and the unquenchable itch to meddle and provoke things, to play tricks on the world and its creatures—these remained unsatisfied.

He had recently stolen the light from the

old man who kept it hidden in a box in his house in the middle of the darkness, and had scattered it throughout the sky. The new light spattered the night with stars and waxed and waned in the shape of the moon. And it dazzled the day with a single bright shining which lit up the long beach that curved from the spit beneath the Raven's feet westward as far as Tao Hill. Pretty as it was, it looked lifeless and so to the Raven quite boring. He gave a great sigh, crossed his wings behind his back and walked along the sand, his shiny head cocked, his sharp eyes and ears alert for any unusual sight or sound. Then taking to the air, he called petulantly out to the empty sky. To his delight, he heard an answering cry—or to describe it more closely, a muffled squeak.

At first he saw nothing, but as he scanned

the beach again, a white flash caught his eye, and when he landed he found at his feet, half buried in the sand, a gigantic clamshell. When he looked more closely still, he saw that the shell was full of little creatures cowering in terror of his enormous shadow.

Well, here was something to break the monotony of his day. But nothing was going to happen as long as the tiny things stayed in the shell, and they certainly weren't coming out in their present terrified state. So the Raven leaned his great head close to the shell, and with the smooth trickster's tongue that had got him into and out of so many misadventures during his troubled and troublesome existence, he coaxed and cajoled and coerced the little creatures to come out and play in his wonderful, shiny new world. As you know, the Raven speaks in two voices, one harsh and strident, and the other, which he used now, a seductive bell-like croon which seems to come from the depth of the sea, or out of the cave where the winds are born. It is an irresistible sound, one of the loveliest sounds in the world. So it wasn't long before one and then another of the little shell-dwellers timidly emerged. Some of them immediately scurried back when they saw the immensity of the sea and the sky, and the overwhelming blackness of the Raven. But eventually curiosity overcame caution and all of them had crept or scrambled out. Very strange creatures they were: two-legged like the Raven, but there the resemblance ended. They had no glossy feathers, no thrusting beak. Their skin was pale, and they were naked except for the long black hair on their round, flat-featured heads. Instead of strong wings, they had thin stick-like appendages that waved and fluttered constantly. They were the original Haidas, the first humans.

For a long time the Raven amused himself with his new playthings, watching them as they explored their much-expanded world. Sometimes they helped one another in their new discoveries. Just as often, they squabbled over some novelty they found on the beach. And the Raven taught them some clever tricks, at which they proved remarkably adept. But the Raven's attention span was brief, and he grew tired of his small companions. For one thing, they were all males. He had looked all up and down the beach for female creatures, hoping to make the game more interesting, but females were nowhere to be found. He was about to shove the now tired, demanding and quite annoying little creatures back into their shell and forget about them when suddenly—as happens so often with the Raven—he had an idea.

He picked up the men, and in spite of their struggles and cries of fright he put them on his broad back, where they hid themselves among his feathers. Then the Raven spread his wings and flew to North Island. The tide was low, and the rocks, as he had expected, were covered with those large but soft-lipped molluscs known as red chitons. The Raven shook himself gently, and the men slid down his back to the sand. Then he flew to the rock and with his strong beak pried a chiton from its surface.

Now, if any of you have ever examined the underside of a chiton, you may begin to understand what the Raven had in his libidinous, devious mind. He threw back his head and flung the chiton at the nearest of the men. His aim was as unerring as only a great magician's can be, and the chiton found its mark in the delicate groin of the startled, shellborn creature. There the chiton attached itself firmly. Then as sudden as spray hitting the rocks from a breaking wave, a shower of chitons broke over the wide-eyed humans, as each of the open-mouthed shellfish flew inexorably to its target.

Nothing quite like this had ever happened to the men. They had never dreamed of such a thing during their long stay in the clamshell. They were astounded, embarrassed, confused by a rush of new emotions and sensations. They shuffled and squirmed, uncertain whether it was pleasure or pain they were experiencing. They threw themselves down on the beach, where a great storm seemed to break over them, followed just as suddenly by a profound calm. One by one the chitons dropped off. The men staggered to their feet and headed slowly down the beach, followed by the raucous laughter of the Raven, echoing all the way to the great island to the north which we now call Prince of Wales.

That first troop of male humans soon disappeared behind the nearest headland, passing out of the games of the Raven and the story of humankind. Whether they found their way back to their shell or lived out their lives elsewhere, or perished in the strange environment in which they found themselves, nobody re-members, and perhaps nobody cares. They had played their roles and gone their way.

Meanwhile the chitons had made their way back to the rock, where they attached themselves as before. But they too had been changed. As high tide followed low and the great storms of winter gave way to the softer rains and warm sun of spring, the chitons grew and grew, many times larger than their kind had ever been before. Their jointed shells seemed about to fly apart from the enormous pressure within them. And one day a huge wave swept over the rock, tore them from their footholds and carried them back to the beach. As the water receded and the warm sun dried the sand, a great stirring began among the chitons. From each emerged a brown-skinned, black-haired human. This time there were both males and females among them, and the Raven could begin his greatest game: one that still goes on.

They were no timid shell-dwellers these, but children of the wild coast, born between the sea and land, challenging the strength of the stormy North Pacific and wresting from it a rich livelihood. Their descendants built on its beaches the strong, beautiful homes of the Haidas and embellished them with the powerful heraldic carvings that told of the legendary beginnings of great families, all the heroes and heroines and the gallant beasts and monsters who shaped their world and their destinies. For many generations they grew and flourished, built and created, fought and destroyed, living according to the changing seasons and the unchanging rituals of their rich and complex lives.

It's nearly over now. Most of the villages are abandoned, and those which have not entirely vanished lie in ruins. The people who remain are changed. The sea has lost much of its richness, and great areas of the land itself lie in waste. Perhaps it's time the Raven started looking for another clamshell.

The Raven and the Big Fisherman

The Raven, most powerful of all the creatures who lived during mythtime, whose whim could light the world and bring the lakes and rivers to Haida Gwaii and fill them with fish, the great transformer of himself and of the universe, the final distillation of the essence of the clever, complex, devious, ingenious restless Haidas—and, for that matter, of all the contradictory human race—the many-voiced and iridescently pitch-black Raven: why is he always walking along some beach, hungry, dissatisfied? Why does he have to resort to trickery of the meanest kind in order to satisfy his desires? Why is he always provoking situations in which even he is very often protected from the ultimate indignity only by the dull device of immortality?

Well, no matter. Here he is again, alone as usual. In mythtime were there other ravens—the ordinary kind we have today, who travel in pairs and chat constantly with each other in their intricate, versatile language? Or did he have no one to talk to but himself? Right now, in this story, he's muttering to himself as he picks his way along, thinking, "Dull beach, all pebbles, hard on the feet, no storm for the past week, nothing washed up on the foreshore fit to eat, rainy again, lonely, hungry, wet, *bored*."

It was then that he saw the house, magnificent against the wet green of the forest: a great

six-beam edifice, with a frontal pole so tall it seemed to pierce the uppermost levels of the rain. The entrance was closed, but smoke rose slowly from the smokehole to mingle with the coastal mist. In a moment, the Raven was flattened against the outside wall, his eye pressed to a crack between the boards, and as he clung to the house in that posture, a most puzzling scene was revealed to him.

The shapes of the beams were almost lost in the shadowy recesses under the huge, high roof, and the excavated floor was so deep that the fire in the centre seemed only a dim glow, no brighter than the pale grey light which seeped down from the distant blur of the smokehole. Yet in spite of its great size, the house seemed almost unoccupied. There were no children running about, no aged aunts or uncles, no young married couples emerging from the alcoves usually to be found along the inner walls of such houses. There was none of the flurry of early morning activity which always begins the day in an extended family dwelling.

Instead, there was a solitary woman stirring the fire and, with her long, wooden tongs, placing hot rocks from the firepit into a wooden box full of water which stood close at hand. As the Raven watched, the water began to steam.

There was only one sleeping alcove visible in the whole house, and it was built against the rear wall, the traditional territory of the family head. The hide curtain closing the alcove was suddenly thrown back, and from behind it stepped the biggest man the Raven—or anyone else, for that matter—had ever seen.

This giant strode to one of the dimly lit corners of the house and returned with a huge storage box, elaborately carved on all sides, glistening with inlaid tiles of colorful abalone shell and closed by a ponderous lid. He set the box down in front of his sleeping quarters, removed the lid and in a deep voice called to his wife to bring him something to drink. But what he asked for was *tang*, which in Haida means seawater.

In the old days it was the custom of the Haidas, before undertaking any great ritual, or entering on any other pursuit which involved great risk or required supernatural aid, to purify themselves by fasting, sexual abstinence, and by external and internal cleansing of the body. The skin was scrubbed with water to which some urine had been added, and the inner organs were cleansed by drinking quantities of warm seawater. This very quickly flushed out the entire digestive tract, leaving the anatomy as unsullied as possible, if also somewhat shaken.

The Raven, watching the woman bring her husband a container of steaming brine, quite naturally assumed that he was going to witness such a ritual cleansing, though he thought it somewhat strange that it should be performed inside the home. The process became more mysterious, however, as the big man swallowed the entire container of seawater at a single gulp, and at once vomited a great river of salt water and half-digested food into the enormous chest in front of him. This was no ordinary regurgitation of the stomach contents, but a rushing torrent which went on and on until it seemed inconceivable that even so huge a body as that of the giant could contain such a volume of fluid.

When the flow ceased at last, the big man rinsed his mouth with more seawater, then arose and took from its peg on the wall of the house an elaborately carved halibut hook and a long skein of cedarbark rope. He attached a stone weight to the hook and, to the Raven's astonishment, lowered it into the chest into which he had just vomited.

Well, the Raven is a carrion bird, not noted for the delicacy of his sensibility nor the fastidiousness of his taste, but even he felt his stomach move somewhat uneasily, as he pondered what the big man might be expecting to catch in such malodorous waters.

His amazement grew as the strange fisherman continued to play out the line, for soon the entire skein, obviously many fathoms long, had gone into the chest. And not until the last fathom was reached did the Raven see the line go slack in the fisherman's hands, showing that his hook had at last touched bottom. Then almost at once the line went taut again, much tauter than before, and agitated besides. As the Raven's eye grew steadily wider behind the crack, the giant rapidly hauled in the line and pulled out of the chest a fine halibut, just the right size to provide the most tasty and delicate flesh.

The Raven had seen many remarkable things in his time, including feats of extraordinary magic, but never had he been so impressed as he was now by the power of another of the creatures of mythtime. It was, after all, not just a convincing display of magical skill; it also promised an endless supply of something dear to the Raven's sinewy, black heart—and that is good food.

He resolved at once to find some way of turning this new discovery to his own advantage, and to that end he continued watching the residents of the strange, gigantic house.

The Big Fisherman, as the Raven decided to call him, started sorting equipment and clothing, as if he were contemplating a journey, and indeed he soon announced to his wife that he planned to be absent for several days. He was going, he said, to an island some distance away, which was known to be the home of a large number of redshafted flickers—whose feathers, as everyone knows, are indispensable to several powerful rituals. The Big Fisherman's wife then busied herself preparing food for his journey, and by this time the Raven had formulated his plan.

He retreated a short distance from the house and concealed himself in the spruce trees. From this position, he was soon able to watch the Big Fisherman load his canoe and paddle off. When the canoe disappeared behind the first headland, the Raven stepped from his place of concealment, but when he did so, he no longer appeared in the form of a rather bedraggled, black bird. Instead, he appeared in every detail to be the Big Fisherman himself. In this guise he walked briskly to the house, pushed the loose plank forward on its leather hinges, and stepped confidently through the doorway.

The Raven is by no means the only creature of the Islands able to change his form so fluently. Another, well known to all Haida mariners, is the Chumaos, or Snag, an ocean creature which may take the form of a floating tree, a house, a ladder, a seabear or any number of other disguises. And whenever you see a Chumaos, you must give no sign that you have seen it. If you stare at it, or make any attempt to follow it, your boat will be swamped in a furious storm.

So the Raven greeted the wife of the Big Fisherman with a simple and wholly credible explanation of her husband's sudden reappearance.

"I saw a Chumaos," he said, "and I didn't recognize it as such until I had looked at it longer than would have been wise. So I decided to put off the search for the feathers. I'll go to the island at a later time.

"But I'm hungry after paddling back so hard to escape the Chumaos," said the Raven. "Heat some more seawater. It's time to go halibut fishing again."

The Raven went into the corner of the huge house and dragged out the chest, just as he had seen the Big Fisherman do that morning. He drank the warm seawater, vomited into the chest, rinsed his mouth, and took the halibut hook and the stone weight from the pegs where they hung on the wall. As soon as he had rigged his tackle and played out the line, he felt a satisfying bite, and a few moments later, he pulled out a magnificent fish. The Big Fisherman's wife cleaned and cooked his catch, and he consumed it with all the voracity for which he and his kind are known.

With his appetite momentarily satisfied, the Raven looked around the house to see what other entertainments he could find, and the first thing his greedy eyes lit upon was of course the Big Fisherman's wife. She was a comely lady indeed, and as the Raven shortly discovered, she was affectionately obliging to his every request, no matter how curious it might seem. And some of them may well have seemed a little curious to the young woman, for the Raven was already a creature of vast experience, who had known the affections of many females of all species during the long, libidinous centuries of his immortality.

For her part, the Fisherman's wife could not remember when her husband had paid her such intimate attention, and she began to have many kind thoughts about the Chumaos whom she believed had forced her husband to return so unexpectedly from his expedition.

It is in the nature of things, though, that the Raven seldom has a completely untroubled time. And as someone was to say much later, no good deed, no matter how well intentioned, ever goes unpunished. The Big Fisherman, after he rounded the second headland, really did encounter a Chumaos. And instead of ignoring it as he should have, he stared for a long time at this monster of the ocean. Only when it started moving toward him, kicking up wind and waves and flashing with lightning, did the Fisherman realize the danger he was in.

Using all his great strength to speed the canoe back through the water, the Big Fisherman managed to escape, but he also decided it was not a good day for a journey to gather red flicker feathers. He returned home instead, to find what was obviously himself already there, locked in a warm embrace with his wife.

If such a thing happened to one of us, in our much more ordinary world, we might have no idea how to proceed. But the Big Fisherman knew very well that there could be only one explanation for his being cuckolded by himself. One of the two of him had to be the Raven, and the one most likely to be the Raven, as the Fisherman well knew, was the one in bed with his wife. So he reached at once for his great fishclub and mercilessly attacked this stranger who looked so convincingly like himself.

It gave him a strange discomfort at first to be doing such violence to his own image, but after a few blows, that image transformed itself into a great black bird, squawking and struggling to take flight. At this, the Big Fisherman attacked all the more furiously. And the smokehole was so far away, and the club so big and the Fisherman so tall, that before the Raven could make his escape he was battered against the walls, the roof and the floor, until all that remained of him was a soggy lump of blood and crushed feathers.

When the Fisherman had convinced himself that no life stirred in this residue of the Raven, he gave his wife a couple of hearty but somewhat less violent swipes with the club as well, just to see whether she too might choose to transform herself into something else. Then he instructed her to clean up the mess and to drop what remained of the Raven into the latrine, making sure that not the smallest fragment of bone, beak or feather remained behind.

She did very dutifully as she was told, but could not help regretting, as she handled the pulped and battered body, that the amorous facsimile of her husband had been changed so quickly to its present form.

Life in the Big Fisherman's house returned to normal—and the truth is, things weren't really so unusual even for the Raven. Lying in fragments in a frequently used latrine was not much worse, and in essence not much different, than many other predicaments in which the Raven has been found. But as his consciousness returned and he examined his new surroundings, the Raven began to ponder why his adventures led so often to such undignified conclusions. He began to question whether it was really worth the effort to retransform himself and carry on. Ideally situated as he was for the contemplation of such matters, he settled in to do some serious thinking instead of venturing directly back into the world.

Later that day, when the Fisherman's wife came out to use the latrine, the Raven realized what he'd been waiting for. Looking up at the very portion of her anatomy to which he had earlier devoted such patient attention, the Raven forgot all about being fed up with his existence. Reassembling one claw and enough of his muscles to move it, he reached upward to grasp the former object of his desires, now hovering just above him. But the Big Fisherman's wife, when she felt the sudden, cold touch of the scaly talons, leaped to her feet and ran screaming back to her husband.

Realizing that this could bring further trouble, the Raven struggled to reassemble his wings, both legs, his head and his tail in proper order so he could escape. The beating had been so severe, however, and the destruction so complete, that before the Raven had himself functioning properly again, the Big Fisherman had returned, this time accompanied by several friends. The group of them dragged the half-reconstituted bird out of the smelly pit and pummelled him back into a mush of shattered bones, torn flesh and crumpled feathers.

They trussed the almost shapeless corpse of the Raven up tightly with cedarbark fishing line, weighted it with heavy rocks and tossed it into their canoe. Then they paddled him far out to sea where they dumped him overboard, into the next story.

The Raven with the Broken Beak

The Raven, or what was left of him—a wad of ruptured organs, crushed bones and broken body parts bound together with fishing line and weighted with heavy stones—sank swiftly into the bottomless trench in the seabed which the Big Fisherman had selected as the likeliest place to dispose of this troublesome creature once and for all.

But of course there was no real danger of that. The Raven is doomed to continue forever his restless wanderings through the world, searching for something to quell his insatiable appetites. Sinking endlessly into a bottomless pit in the sea is a fate no worse than many others, but the Raven knew he must put it behind him sooner or later. So instead of vanishing into the infinite depths of the ocean, from which it could be laborious to emerge, the Raven transformed himself quickly once more. With tremendous effort, he reconstituted the broken shreds of his body, rebuilding them not into his usual glossy black shape, but into the form of a silver-bright, sleek spring salmon.

With a quick shake of his lithe new body, he was able to free himself of the fishing line and the stones. He began at once swimming back upward toward the world of sunlight and air—the world in which, like the rest of his kind, he was most comfortable and with which he was most familiar.

Nearing the bright canopy of waves, the Raven was contemplating quite cheerfully his immediate prospects and savouring memories of the pleasanter parts of his recent adventures. These thoughts occupied him sufficiently that he failed to notice the huge black-and-white form of the great hunter, one of the lords of the watery universe, a *sghaana*, or killer whale, bearing swiftly down upon him. When he felt the great jaws open behind him at last, escape was clearly impossible. In the final moment before the teeth clashed shut upon him, he turned and swam up the long black tunnel of the throat, into the cavernous belly of the whale.

Seeing that his salmon shape had clearly outlived its usefulness, the Raven resumed his usual form—eyes, beak, feathers and claws all as black as the starless night in which he was born.

It was warm and, for a moment, somewhat restful deep in the body of the killer whale. It was better than lying, trussed up in fishing line, in the bottom of the Big Fisherman's canoe, and certainly better than being bitten in half and chewed. But when his eyes began to smart and the ends of his feathers to wilt and fray in the strong stomach acids of the whale, the Raven concluded it was time to leave. Drawing, therefore, on his most basic natural powers, he pecked and clawed his way through the walls of the whale's belly and out through the layers of muscle, blubber and hide.

After all this profitless activity, one would think that the Raven would stop for nothing on his way back to his natural element. But the

Raven is not an altogether prudent sort of bird, and after the unexpected labor of chewing a hole in the side of the whale, the Raven had been reminded that he was hungry. So when a tasty-looking bit of octopus tentacle drifted by, as it did just then, within easy range of his beak, he reached out and grabbed it.

He should have suspected, of course, that a carefully cut and skinned section of octopus tentacle floating near the seafloor might not have been placed there for the express delectation of underwater ravens hatched from the bellies of passing killer whales. All things considered, he ought to have looked the piece of tentacle over quite carefully before gobbling it down—but when food is at hand, the Raven often forgets such precautions.

So he failed to notice the strip of kelp leading down to the stone sinker on the ocean floor below the tentacle, and he failed to notice the second strand of kelp leading up from the stone toward the surface. He failed to notice the hook, too, until the barb stabbed suddenly into his upper beak and his body was flooded with pain.

This pain was compounded a moment later, as the Raven was suddenly flipped on his back and began to lurch helplessly toward the surface. He had been caught, as he now knew, by one of the ingenious halibut hooks of the Haidas, which flip the fish over as soon as the hook sets and tension is put on the line. In this way, the flow of water over the gills is reversed, and before it is drawn to the surface, the halibut drowns.

If the Raven, so skilled as he is at holding

his breath, was himself in no great danger of drowning, he was nevertheless in excruciating pain, and he could expect in a few more moments to be at the mercy of mere human beings, and to suffer still further humiliation and pain at their hands. When he saw that the current had brought him in reach of a kelp bed, he lunged for one of the largest stalks and hung onto it fiercely with his claws. The halibut fishermen in their canoe struggled meanwhile to bring in their suddenly obstinate catch, and a vigorous tug-of-war ensued. Neither Raven nor fisherman nor fishline nor kelpstalk would yield, and at last the whole upper beak of the desperate bird was torn out of his face by its roots and jerked toward the surface.

The Raven clung to the kelp for some moments in agony, wondering how he would ever be able to eat properly again. Then he rose to the surface at last and flew high into the air, watching the fishermen paddle away. He followed them to their camp in a small cove where they beached their canoe and kindled a fire. Once he was satisfied they would be there all evening, he flew back out to sea in the fading light, looking for anything that would help him recover his beak, and when his sharp ears heard it, he knew what he was seeking: the mournful peal of the wounded killer whale.

Flying in short circles over the stricken animal, the Raven spoke to him in tones of great sympathy.

"Alath, my poor friend," said the Raven with the broken beak, "I thee that you altho are in great dithtreth, and I fear that if both of uth do not get help we will quickly perith.

"I am going now to the houthe of a great thaman, whothe powerth I have ekthperienthed before. You may follow me if you with, and I will athk him to treat you too."

The astonished whale thanked the Raven profusely and readily agreed.

"He ith ekthpecting me only," said the Raven. "Wait a little dithtanth offthyore, and I will tell him you are there. If he agreeth to treat you, I will thignal you by throwing dry thedar onto the fire."

Again the suffering whale agreed.

"When you thee the fire blathe up, you mutht come athyore. The thaman can only treat you on the beach. You mutht thwim right up through the thallowth and onto the gravel, ath clothe ath pothible to the fire."

And so desperate, yet so hopeful, was the

whale, that he agreed unquestioningly even to these instructions.

The Raven perched on his dorsal fin, guiding him toward the camp, and when they came up opposite the cove, where the fire could be clearly seen, the whale slowed.

"Wait here," said the Raven to the whale, and he flew alone to the edge of the beach.

As he landed, he transformed himself once more, now taking the form of a shrivelled little human being. Even in human form, he was missing his nose and most of his palate. To obscure this deformity, he transformed the cloak of feathers into an oversized spruceroot hat, which covered his whole face and most of his upper body, and in this guise he started toward the fire.

The fishermen, who had finished their evening meal, sat in a half circle around the flames, with their backs to the gentle evening breeze. They were discussing the day's events and passing from hand to hand the strange black object they had pulled up out of the ocean. Each offered his own opinion of the catch, but in spite of their vast knowledge of the sea, not one of them could identify what it was, and none had a guess which seemed convincing to the others.

They were about to give up the discussion, for it was time to turn in for the night, when they heard slow footsteps coming toward them over the beach gravel. A small, wizened man—or at least they thought it was probably human—wearing a huge spruceroot hat and leaning on a walking stick, stepped into view in the dwindling firelight.

"I think I know what you have there," said a strange voice which came from under the hat, "but I'll have to ekthamine it clothely to be thyure."

Though he was small enough to seem harmless, such a suspicious looking creature, arriving so late at night, would normally have drawn a hostile reaction from the men around the fire. But his offer to answer the question which had perplexed them for several hours was enough that they invited him to sit down. One of them handed the visitor the beak, and he seemed to study it with great care.

"Yeth, I think tho," said the Raven. "Throw thome of that dry thedar on the fire, tho I can thee thith object more clearly."

The fisherman nearest the woodpile grabbed an armload of dry cedar sticks and tossed them onto the fire.

"Jutht ath I thought," said the Raven as the fresh flames rose. "I have theen one of theeth before, and it wath a bad day indeed for thothe who found it. Like you, they pathed it from hand to hand ath they that round the fire, contaminating themthelvth with the evil magic it contained. That night, though it wath ath calm ath it ith now, a great monthter came thuddenly out of the thea. It dethtroyed their camp, their canoeth, and killed everyone ekthept me. I wath wounded, but I thurvived becauthe I fled into the foretht to hide. If I had run farther into the treeth, I might not have been injured, but I wath curiouth. I thtopped and looked back for a moment, and the monthter'th power touched me."

As the Raven finished speaking, the beach behind him erupted with flying pebbles and spray. Using the last of his strength, the killer whale flung himself up on the gravel, roaring in agony at those gathered around the fire.

The fishermen leaped to their feet and ran into the forest, not once looking back, and the Raven chuckled maliciously as he heard the confused sounds of their frantic thrashing recede. Reassuming his natural form, he slid the beak back into place, and in moments it knitted there, strong and sound as though it had known no injury.

Thus equipped, and completely at leisure, he gorged himself on the ample supply of fresh halibut which the fishermen had left behind—and on the tasty and unharmed pieces of octopus tentacle which he found in their bait box. Temporarily satisfied, he flew off, bidding a contemptuous, lisping farewell to the dying whale.

As dawn broke, the fishermen made their way cautiously back to the beach, where they found their fire dead, their catch eaten or spoiled, and the stranger gone. A sad morning indeed, had they not also found on the beach, stranded by the falling tide, the dead killer whale.

The Haidas never hunted the whale themselves, but from that morning to this, they have eaten its flesh with great pleasure whenever they find a fresh killer whale carcass on shore.

So quite inadvertently once again, in the undivided pursuit of his calling—in the relentlessness of his search for amusement and food—the Raven had brought a little pleasure, a little profit and even some knowledge to his favorite playthings, human beings.

The Bear Mother and
Her Husband

The greatest of all the sagas of the Northwest
Coast people is the tragic, noble tale of the
Bear Mother and the founding of the Bear
family of the Raven side of the clan groupings
of the Haidas. And yet it begins in a prosaic
way, with a rather bad tempered, flighty, head-
strong girl who wore the privileges of her high
rank with scant grace and little compassion.

In the old days, when the time came to harvest and preserve the seasonal foods, rank was largely put aside, and the highest born worked beside the lowliest slave to assure a plentiful supply of all that the rich land provided. The salmonberries were ripening in profusion at the time when this story begins, and the young woman had no trouble in filling her basket, in spite of the fact that her mind was anywhere and everywhere but on the mundane business of berry picking.

It was a beautiful, warm day, and she was dreaming of the new life about to begin for her—for she had overheard her parents planning her marriage and had seen the envoys from some of the great Eagle families come to bring gifts. She hoped her parents would choose some young man who had no other

wives, but she knew she would have to accept whatever was considered the most advantageous alliance.

In any case, she was happily anticipating the increased prestige she would have as the wife of a powerful man. And just as the vision of herself in new robes, sharing pride of place at some great feast, was growing so real she could almost taste the food and hear the beat of the drums and the singing of the people, the young woman stepped into a pile of bearshit, slipped and fell, soiling herself thoroughly and spilling every last one of her berries.

Back in mythtime, when all this took place, relations between the bears and the humans were not very close, but then they were not unfriendly either. The two species tolerated each other, and when an encounter took place each largely ignored the other, pretending to have some important business to attend to in the opposite direction, very much as they do today. There is no record of any injury being done to a human by a bear in the Haida Islands. Unfortunately, the reverse is not quite as true, but on the whole bears and people have always lived there on reasonably cordial terms.

So the angry screams of the girl, describing the bear whom she held responsible for her indignity, and all his near relations, and of course his entire ancestry, in the most derogatory, unflattering terms she could summon from her rich and colorful language, formed a major break in the longstanding tradition.

It certainly didn't go unnoticed by the pair of bears who were feeding contentedly nearby on the same salmonberries the young woman had been gathering. And they had no trouble understanding what she was saying, for in those days the animals all had both human and animal forms, and they understood the ways and the language of humans very well.

When they heard the tirade of insults, they rushed to the spot where our heroine was still trying to recover from her ignominious mishap, and they seized her roughly, paying no attention whatever to her cries, her noble birth, nor to the unspoken pact between her people and theirs. They dragged her off to their village, where they threw her into a small, shed-like structure, windowless, with a dirt floor, no smokehole and only one entrance. This they closed tightly behind her with a large rock.

The girl made no attempt then to escape. She knew that even if she found a way out, the magic of the bears would soon bring her back—and in any case, she could not take her place in her village again, after having been captured by her hairy assailants. So she curled up on the cold earth, feeling very sorry for herself and wondering what was going to happen to her next. She began to weep softly, and as she contemplated further the hopelessness of her condition, her weeping became an uncontrolled sobbing.

In the midst of a particularly heartrending cry, she thought she heard a little, squeaky voice from a corner of her prison, and it seemed to say, "Now, now, my girl, that's no way to carry on. You're in a very tough situation, thanks mainly to your own vain arrogance. But let's see if there's something we can do."

As the little voice went on, it seemed to

grow closer and louder, accompanied by a slight scratchy sound. Nevertheless it was quite a shock for the girl to feel on her leg the touch of a tiny, cold, sharp-nailed hand or foot or claw, and to realize that the creature speaking out of the blackness was right beside her.

"Who are you and where did you come from and what's going to happen to me now?"

"My name is Qaganjat. You can call me Mouse Woman—and I happen to have run entirely out of mountain goat tallow, which I'm very fond of indeed. I also happen to know young girls like you often carry some with you to use on your faces. Do you have any with you now?"

"Yes," said the girl somewhat unwillingly.

"Well you won't be needing it here. Would you like to make me a present of some of it?"

"Yes," said the girl, just as unwillingly. And

she brought out a small nugget of mountain goat tallow which she carried tucked in her hair.

"Thank you," said Mouse Woman, in her small, cool voice. "Now, my dear, to be quite candid, you're in a great deal of trouble. You could sit here for a long, long time until those bears decide what to do with you. Or they could make you a slave right away, and that wouldn't be such a good thing either, because they've had no practice in dealing with human slaves. They might work you too hard. Who knows? They might kill you. They might even eat you. But I have an idea that could get us around all that. You're a chief's daughter. You must have a copper bracelet. And copper is a sacred metal among the bears just as it is among the humans. That's how we'll do it."

The Mouse Woman instructed the girl to break her bracelet in half. The girl objected strongly to this, saying the bracelet had been given to her at her puberty rites, that she must respect it and those who had given it to her, and that she'd lose status the moment the bracelet was broken.

"That's all very well," said Mouse Woman squeakily. "But your status won't do you much good if they kill you, will it? And if they don't kill you, but only make you a slave, you'll have no status anyhow, will you?"

So the girl did as she was told and awaited further instructions.

"Sooner or later somebody out there will remember that you need something to eat," said the Mouse Woman, "and they'll have to remove the stone to give you the food. When they do, tell them you have to empty your bowels. They'll let you out to do that, though they'll keep a close watch on you. So you'll have to be very careful about what you do. Without letting the bears see you do it, dig a small hole for your waste, and cover it over as soon as you're finished. Then take half of your bracelet and leave it on the ground where you've been, and we'll see what happens."

The girl did as Mouse Woman told her and was soon returned to her prison. A whole day passed, and nothing happened as far as she could tell, but in the bear village, and particularly in the house of the chief of the bears, there were great discussions and speculations. As soon as they had seen their captive deposit a shining piece of copper where they had expected ordinary body waste, the bear guards had rushed to their leader carrying the news and the incontestable evidence: the broken half of the bracelet.

Intrigued by this unexpected occurrence, the chief instructed the guards to watch the girl even more closely. When food was brought to her once again the next morning, she repeated her request to be allowed to relieve herself, and again accomplished the substitution of copper for human waste, using the remaining half of the bracelet.

On the presentation of this second piece of evidence, the chief of the bears was fully convinced that he had a most unusual captive, and he ordered the guards to bring the girl before him.

As soon as she entered his house, he invited her to share his lavishly carved seat with him.

"It is clear, gracious lady, that you, who can transform slaves' food into copper, the most precious substance in the world, through the natural workings of your undoubtedly magical body, are a personage of very exceptional qualities and must belong to one of the great families of the humans. Please accept the heartfelt apologies of myself and my people for the treatment you've received from some of the younger and ruder members of my family. We will do everything in our power to atone for these insults to your highborn person."

To this, the girl immediately replied that the only thing she wanted from the bears was to be returned to her own people.

"Of course, that can be arranged whenever you wish," the chief assured her, "but first we have some insignificant, valueless gifts we hope you will accept, and which may compensate in a small way for the indignities we have done to you in our ignorance and our quite unjustified anger."

A parade of bear people then approached the chief and his guest, each of the bears carrying a beautifully wrought object. One held a handsomely carved bowl, another a gracefully shaped horn spoon, another a spruceroot basket, and the last a robe of the choicest, deepest, thickest bearskin you can imagine.

As we said at the beginning of the story, this young woman was not without vanity. She was not without greed, either, and as the pile of presents grew, she began to think much more kindly of her captors. And when at their urging she tried on the robe, a strange feeling came over her. The bears, who had until then seemed terribly alien to her, and frightening, suddenly seemed more acceptable, even familiar. She saw that they weren't, as she'd thought, all the same, but that they were male and female, old and young, bright and foolish, attractive and . . . what was she thinking of? Bears *attractive*? And yet that young male approaching her now did indeed have something that set him apart from the others. . . .

While these thoughts crackled suddenly in her head, she heard, as from a great distance, the voice of the chief saying something about his nephew: how he would someday inherit the chief's rank and wealth, how he should be married by now, but that it had so far proved impossible to find him a bride of sufficient standing, and that perhaps she would consider. . . .

As she realized at last where the bear chief's talk was leading, she began vehemently to think how unthinkable and say how unspeakable was the whole idea. But as the chief, taking no notice of her objections, continued quietly, pointing out the handsome young bear man in front of her as the very nephew of whom he was speaking, she allowed herself at least to discuss the possibility. And as the talk wore on, and she grasped that the chief of the bears, despite the unfailing courtesy of his speech, had no intention at all of returning her to her people, finally, reluctantly, having held out for everything she thought she could possibly get in the circumstances, the girl consented to marry the handsome young bear.

And so, the myth tells us, the marriage took place, even though the circumstances were what may politely be called extremely unusual. It's not too often that bears and humans marry—yet that in itself perhaps poses no insurmountable problem. But for members of two noble families—whether humans or bears—to be united with only one of those families present is, in Haida tradition, unthinkable.

Let us, therefore, not think of it, nor attempt to unravel any details, but merely accept that some sort of ceremony took place, after which the couple settled down to a married existence as normal as possible under these conditions.

As a married couple, they became heads of their own household yet shared with their extended family a single substantial dwelling. The young husband turned out to be as kind and gentle as his bride had hoped, and the girl, as she assumed her position in the bear community, soon cast aside the frivolous, selfish behavior of her younger days and became a respected member of the tribe.

Most of the time she was happy enough, growing more fond of her husband as the days went on and finding her other bear relatives tolerable, sometimes interesting companions—not much different, in fact, from the humans she had left behind. Yet her separation from her old friends, and especially from her family, prevented her entering fully into the life of her new community. From time to time homesickness overcame her, and her sorrow was felt by those close to her, especially her husband. The two of them sometimes passed days in a gloomy silence.

At times such as these, the woman took her bearskin cloak from its richly carved storage box and wrapped it around her. Deep in the folds of the robe, she seemed to forget much of her sorrow at being separated from her family and from humankind.

And then one day she realized she was going to become a mother. From then until the time of the birth, she was so busy worrying about what her offspring would look like that she had little time for homesickness.

She gave birth, after a very difficult labor, to twin sons—as far as anyone could tell, perfect bear cubs, untainted by any human characteristics. Strangely enough, this didn't distress their mother at all, and from the moment they were born she lavished on them as much love and affection as if they had been her own kind. Yet she did often wish they weren't so rough when she was nursing them.

The cubs grew, and life went on, and it looked as though their father would in due time take his place as head of the clan. It looked, in fact, as though the episode of human intrusion into the bear village would soon become merely a half-forgotten incident in the long history of the bears.

The purpose of myths, however, is not merely to relate experiences, but to lead to significant changes in the structure of things. So this peaceful condition could hardly continue indefinitely.

The first indication of the disruption soon to take place was mild enough: merely the sound of dogs in the far distance. But on the following day when the sound was heard again, now apparently much closer, a feeling of apprehension ran through the whole of the bear community. The once flighty young woman, now the affectionate and respected Bear Mother of this story, grew deeply anxious and yet excited at the sound, for she recognized the barking and knew that the dogs were those of her brothers. Half of her feared for the safety of her husband and her children, and for the welfare of her new family and friends, but the other half felt a renewed desire to return to her own people. Such is the power of a barking dog.

The woman confided her suspicions to her husband, who reported them in turn to his uncle, the chief of the bears, and the old chief called a council of the elders to consider what should be done. The last thing the bears wanted was enmity between themselves and human beings, and so, reluctantly, they decided that, to preserve the peace, the Bear Mother and her husband and their children would have to be sent into exile.

The family departed at once and travelled as fast as possible, but every day the howling of the dogs grew louder and closer behind them. The woman and her cubs were soon at the point of exhaustion, and even the Bear Father himself was growing weary under this steady pursuit. When they came to a cave, they determined to remain there in the hope that it might conceal them, and at least give them some respite from the chase. But on the following day they heard the hunters and their dogs gathered directly outside the cave.

The Bear Father knew then that his destiny

was almost fulfilled. He instructed his wife to go to her brothers and tell them that, for the Bear clan of the humans to be established among the Haidas, they must promise not to smoke him out of his den, as humans might with an ordinary bear—but that they must wait until the following day, when he would emerge and, in ceremonial combat with the brothers, would allow himself to be killed.

With great sorrow, yet also conscious of the role she was playing in the future of her family, the Bear Mother followed her husband's instructions and obtained the agreement of her brothers. Then she returned to spend a last night in the cave.

On the following morning, singing his death song, which he commanded his enemies to learn, the Bear Father left the shelter of the cave, and in the unequal combat that followed, he was killed by his wife's brothers.

The Bear Mother and her cubs returned to her village, where the brothers took the bear as their crest. The cubs, after sampling life as lived by the humans, decided that being bears was much preferable. Both of them soon left their mother's village forever, and returned to the house of their grandfather and uncles. But the Bear Mother in time resumed her place in the human community, where she remarried and gave birth to a number of offspring— these, of course, entirely human.

Her eldest human son, in accordance with Haida matrilineal tradition, became the heir of his older maternal uncle, one of the hunters. So the Bear Mother's human children carried on the Bear clan, one of the most numerous and powerful groups among the Haidas. During their great days, many of the poles, and countless other objects of ceremonial value in the Haida villages, were carved with images of the Bear. And members of the Bear clan, though they hunted the bear for his flesh as well as his hide, did so with deep reverence, expressed in elaborate ritual, always including the death song which they learned from their great ancestor.

But as the old tellers of the myth would sometimes say, *hao tlan l ghiida*: now it comes to an end.

Nanasimgit and His Wife

When he was young he lived in a brushwood shack at the edge of the village. His mother had vanished, his uncles were dead, no one knew who his father was. He lived there alone with his grandmother. She and the great blue heron with the cracked beak, whom he met while he was still a child, taught him everything he knew.

And they taught him well, so when he grew older, he could get game when nobody else could, and could catch large halibut when others caught nothing but undersized cod. In a

few years, he was able to build a good house, as large as anyone else's. Then he was waiting to have the right figures to put on the pole.

His clansmen began to be much more polite to him then, and they kept their most beautiful daughters at home, in hopes he might marry them. But none of the girls of the village pleased him, and after a time he said he would look for a wife among the daughters of the others, who live inside the sea. He laid up a store of smoked fish and oil and wood for his grandmother. Then one night he disappeared.

A year later, a strange canoe arrived at the village, and the young hunter sat in the bow. Carved chests full of food, copper jewelry, blankets and hides were unloaded, and a small cloud sat among the boxes. People gathered on the shore, looking at him and asking where he had been.

He went up to the house and greeted his grandmother.

"Grandmother, will you go down and bring up my wife?"

She went down to the beach, but returned alone and said, "Grandson, no one is there. I see nothing but boxes. And resting among the boxes is a little cloud."

"That is my wife," said the hunter. "Will you invite her in?"

His grandmother went back to the beach and spoke to the cloud.

"Come up to the house, daughter-in-law," she said, and the cloud followed her through the door and came close to the hunter.

Guests were gathering, looking for his wife.

He said to the cloud, "Will you take off your hat?"

"You take it off," a voice said to him softly.

He touched the cloud and set it behind him. They could see her then, sitting where the cloud had been. And those who had wanted to marry him, and those who had wanted their daughters to marry him, stared at her and wept. She was that pretty.

He and his wife settled into the large house that he had built, sharing it with his grandmother. Soon after that, he set out to hunt seals.

As he was leaving, his grandmother said to him, "Could it be snowing there in the kelp bed?"

He looked back at the water and there, bobbing in the kelp, he saw a snow white form.

He gave no further thought to seals, but went straight for the kelp bed, chasing the white sea otter. All that day he stalked it in his canoe, and when he speared it at last, he speared it under the tail, so the pelt would carry no scar.

His grandmother skinned it, working the knife with great care, but when she had finished, there was one spot of blood on the fur.

"Let me clean it," his wife said.

She walked out on the point with it, where there were clear pools, free of sand, in the surf-polished rock. There she slipped on the wet stone, and the otter pelt fell in the sea.

She jumped in to retrieve it, and just as she touched it, the black shape of a killer whale rose from beneath her, lifting her clear of the waves. She clung to his dorsal fin and he carried her away.

The hunter chased after her in his canoe, but he found nothing at the spot where the whale had dived, and he waited in vain for his wife or the whale to surface again.

He returned to the village to fast for four days. Then he drank devil's club juice and ate cornlily leaves till the wind blew right through him. On the fifth day, he bathed in aged urine and gathered the things he might need: a mussel shell knife, twisted cedar limbs, goat hair, a whetstone, a comb and dried bearberry leaves.

With these, he returned to the spot where the whale had gone down. There he moored the canoe to a two-headed kelp, gathered up all the items he had brought with him, took one great breath, and dived.

On the floor of the sea lay a trail, which he

followed, and not far along it he met four geese. Their eyes would not open, but they had the keen nostrils of the blind.

"I smell Nanasimgit," one said.

"Me too," said another.

"I also smell Nanasimgit," said a third.

"Then that is my name," said the hunter.

With his mussel shell knife he slit open the sealed lids of the eyes of the three geese who had spoken, and each of them thanked him profusely. But the fourth goose said, "No, I don't want to see it. I don't want to see it!"

Instead of unsealing the last one's eyes, the hunter picked her some goose grass. Then all the geese were grateful.

"I am looking for my wife," he said.

"She came this way," said the geese. "Go farther along and speak to the Heron."

The hunter, wearing his new name, walked down the trail. There he met the Heron, who was repairing a cracked canoe.

"*Hlghaa*," said the Heron.

"Nanasimgit," said the hunter, and he tossed into the Heron's mouth a large pinch of bearberry leaves.

The Heron chewed these reflectively.

"You may find these useful for the canoe," said Nanasimgit, giving the Heron the twisted cedar limbs.

"Come here," said the Heron, and he caught Nanasimgit up with his wing.

"Hide in my armpit," said the Heron.

A watchman with wooden legs came up the trail.

"I heard you cry out," said the watchman. "What have you seen?"

"Nothing," said the Heron. "I finally found cedar limbs."

"Where would you find twisted cedar limbs here in the sea?" asked the watchman. Then he started sniffing.

"You smell of human being," he said, and he circled the Heron once, then twice, but found nothing.

"That is my own odor," said the Heron. "*Hlghaa!*" And his wings went up suddenly. Nanasimgit barely held on.

"Bearberry leaves!" said the watchman. He reached into the Heron's beak and took some, putting them into his own mouth, and started back down the trail.

The Heron raised his wings again, and Nanasimgit dropped to the ground. He held out a fresh pinch of bearberry leaves.

"Your wife is in the house," said the Heron.

"She is to marry the Killer Whale as soon as she has a fin. Down the trail a little farther, a slave is splitting kindling. Perhaps you can help him."

Nanasimgit went on until he came to the woodpile. A slave was splitting kindling, using a red snapper's tail for a wedge. Nanasimgit watched intently as he struck it with his maul, and the wedge broke. The slave began weeping.

"What's the matter?" asked Nanasimgit.

"The master will beat me," the slave said. "I've broken his wedge."

"Let me see it," said Nanasimgit, as he stepped from behind the woodpile.

He put the broken wedge-end into his mouth and sucked it. It came out whole. Then he gave the slave a pinch of bearberry leaves.

"Have you seen my wife?" asked Nanasimgit.

"She is in the house," said the slave. "I am

splitting this kindling to build the fire to steam a fin for her so she can marry the Killer Whale."

"I want her back," said Nanasimgit.

"When the fire is built, I will take in the water for steaming the fin," said the slave. "I will trip, spilling the water into the fire. When the room fills with steam, run in and take her. She sits on the far side, across from the door."

Nanasimgit hid near the stream. When the slave came for water, he followed him to the door, and when the slave spilled the water and steam filled the house, Nanasimgit rushed in. As he raced out again with his wife, the slave swelled like a bullfrog, blocking the others from getting out the door.

Nanasimgit raced all the way back past the Heron and back past the geese before the killer whales escaped from the house and closed in on him. Then he threw down the goat hair he carried, and a forest sprang up at his heels. He and his wife ran on down the trail to the two-headed kelp and climbed up to the canoe.

When the killer whales closed in again, he threw out the whetstone. Where it hit the water, an island formed. When they closed in again, he threw out the comb, which turned into a reef. When the killer whales came round it, the canoe had already reached the beach, and Nanasimgit and his wife were nowhere to be seen. There was no one at all to be seen, in fact, except Nanasimgit's grandmother, who sat near the house, smiling faintly to herself, stretching and tanning a snow white skin.

The Wasgo and Three Killer Whales

His mother-in-law was convinced he was a lazy good-for-nothing, and maybe it was true. He used to come home late from whatever he did all day, when everyone else was already in bed, and sit in a corner tearing off pieces of dried salmon, or *tsihlji*, with his teeth. It seemed he was too lazy even to poke up the fire. And at the sound of his eating the dried fish, his mother-in-law would roll over and mutter, just loud enough for everyone to hear, "There's my son-in-law, splitting cedar even at this hour, a man who never stops working."

She chided him constantly, in fact, for sleeping too late, for not taking proper care of his tools, for not bringing in enough firewood, and above all, for not catching enough fish or trapping enough game.

He finally grew tired of her nagging and announced he was going inland for several days. "Ha!" said the old lady. "He wants us to think he's actually going out hunting!"

He said nothing to that, but took his best stone adze and his wild crabapple maul and his wedges and one or two other things and set off. He didn't go far—only to the lake a short distance back of the village, but he knew he

would be alone. No one else ever went to the lake anymore, because of the stories of people who'd gone there and just disappeared.

He went directly to a tall red cedar which grew beside the lake, and in a very short time—for he was a strong man, and in spite of what his mother-in-law said, he kept his tools beautifully honed—he had cut through the trunk and dropped the cedar into the lake. Walking far out on the floating trunk, he cut it off at the first limbs. Then he set snares on the hillside and captured hundreds of wrens, for although they are very small, their sinews are the strongest material in the world. He braided these sinews into a long rope and bound it around the butt end of the cedar log. Then he drove wedges into the upper end, splitting the log all the way down to the wren-

sinew binding. Finally he felled a tall, straight alder, and from its trunk cut a stout pole. Then he pried the end of the split redcedar apart like a huge pair of cook's tongs, wedging the split log open with the alderwood pole. And he tied a length of strong line to the alder.

That night he went back to his house in the village and rummaged in the storage chest for more of the wind-dried fish to munch on. A voice out of the darkness said, "There's that son-in-law of mine, hard at work as usual. Did you catch anything, son-in-law?"

He said nothing.

Next day he returned to the lake with a fishing line and caught two large trout. These he suspended between the open jaws of the split cedar.

Shortly, the water of the lake began to

churn, and the head and finned forelegs of the
Seawolf, whom some call the Wasgo, appeared
near the surface. As the huge beast rose
through the open trap, snapping at the bait,
the waiting hunter yanked on the line, dislodg-
ing the alderwood pole, and the split cedar
snapped shut on the monster, breaking its
back. In spite of this injury, the Seawolf
snarled and pawed and thrashed. Twice it
pulled the entire cedar log under but was unable to work itself free. Then the log went
under again, and for long moments the lake
roiled and heaved with eddies and swells.
When the trap floated back to the surface the
third time, the Wasgo hung in it limp and
dazed.

The hunter ran out along the log and drove
his spear, with its tip of sharpened mussel

shell, deep into the body of the Wasgo until no sign whatever of its enormous vitality remained. Then he dragged it ashore, skinned it, and burned the carcass in a great fire.

It was late that night, and the Seawolf's hide was folded and stored in a treebranch, when the hunter returned again to his house for another meal of dried salmon.

His mother-in-law rolled over in bed, looking mockingly at his empty hands. "And what did you catch this time, son-in-law?" she asked.

Again he said nothing.

When he went back to the lake the next day, he removed the Wasgo hide from the tree and wrapped it around himself, smoothing it carefully over his own skin until every wrinkle was gone. He flexed the claws and the fins and the jaws and the tail, and when he was satisfied, he plunged into the water.

The lake was as deep as everyone said it was, and the deeper he swam, the more the rock opened before him until he found himself in the sea.

All that night, he swam up and down the inlet in front of the village. After a time, he caught a large halibut, which he brought ashore and laid at the entryway of the house in which he lived with his wife and his mother-in-law. Then he swam back to the lake, climbed onto the bank and put the Wasgo skin back in the tree. He arrived home in his human form just before morning and lay down to sleep, but was soon awakened by the querulous voice of his mother-in-law announcing to the world that her prayers had brought her a halibut larger than any she had ever seen.

Toward evening that day, the hunter again went back to the lake and put on the skin. Next morning, his mother-in-law found at her door not one but two halibut. She was proud—so proud that her son-in-law had trouble getting any sleep that day, as she strode through the house exclaiming how lucky they all were that she was in touch with the masters of wealth who live in the sea.

Next morning it was not two halibut but three. Then it was a seal, then two seals, then three. The hunter's mother-in-law was by this time convinced that she was able to conjure food from the ocean, and as her pride increased, so did her contempt for her son-in-law.

The following morning, the Wasgo's catch was a killer whale.

The old woman had little choice then but to host a feast, which she announced would take place in two days' time. All that day she could be heard about the house, gesturing to the walls and muttering to the corner posts, preparing a speech in praise of herself for conjuring up the whale.

The morning after that, two whales lay dead on the beach in front of her house, and her pride knew no bounds. She began to think that, if only her daughter were single, the nephews of great chiefs would be coming soon to seek for her hand. She began, moreover, to think that the power of her prayers would be great enough to achieve this very end.

The next day was the day of the feast, and

no fish whatever lay on the beach that morning. The old woman fretted over this for no more than a moment, for she had noticed another good sign. She had not heard her son-in-law munching dried fish in the dark, and he was not there in his bed that morning.

The guests had arrived and the celebrations were well underway—in fact, the old woman had just finished giving her speech—when a great commotion was heard offshore. As the hostess and guests peered through the door and the cracks in the walls, the Wasgo strode up the beach with three freshly killed whales.

The old woman's daughter ran toward the beast, with the guests and her mother close on her heels. And all of them stood there staring in perfect astonishment into the wide black eyes of the Wasgo, for in each eye you could see, unmistakably, the face of the layabout son-in-law. To their many questions, the Wasgo said nothing, and the eyes in his eyes were impassive, though perhaps to the old woman the monster seemed to be grinning.

No one brought fish to the hunter's mother-in-law again, for she fainted and died on the spot. But whales and seals and fish appeared at the door of the old woman's daughter, they say, every morning, winter and summer, for the rest of her days.

The Eagle and the Frog

The Raven, who thought nothing of stealing rivers and streams by the thousand, and who lay with many another man's wife and many an innocent girl without risking his own heart—indeed, without breaking anything deeper or tenderer than his beak—the same Raven who created the difference between the sexes in the first place by mating the delicate lips of the chiton with the long, curious muscle of the clam, all for a joke, leaving others to suffer the endless peculiar effects of his invention, the Raven himself, in one of his many incarnations, fell deeply in love one day. He fell in love with a mainland stream, a sonorous, cool, sundappled, clear-running creek whom he happened to meet when she was dallying on her private mainland beach in the form of a beautiful young woman.

Her nails were pure, solid copper. A live hummingbird nuzzled her hair, and she carried a stick adorned with another live creature, the one the Haidas call the forest crab: a frog.

Something he had never quite known came over the Raven. Assuming his own most respectable human form, he begged the woman before him to marry him—and she, to the Raven's unfeigned, unconcealed delight, accepted his offer. When the marriage feast was over, the Raven returned with his bride to the Islands, where he built her a fine house made

entirely of water, in an area known as Ghao-qons, or Big Bay. On modern charts it is shown as Gillatt Arm, off Cumshewa Inlet, on the northeast coast of Moresby Island.

She may not have seen her husband much, for he had plenty of business elsewhere, and as relentless a curiosity after his marriage as before, but the wife of the Raven lived many years in Ghaoqons, until, in this century, she was driven underground by the clear-cut logging of her watershed—with what results we do not yet altogether know, though we can surmise. The old people knew very well that she, like the other Creek Women of the Islands, did not take insults lightly.

As the Raven was a Raven, so his wife was of the other side, the Eagle side, of the Haidas. Among her descendants was a young princess named Wealthsound. When we meet her in this story, however, Wealthsound is a long way from home, and is looking anything but regal. She had tramped many days alone through the forest. Her hair was matted, her clothes torn, her feet bloody and muddy and blistered and sore. Yet you might have known her for a princess even so, by her speech and her bearing perhaps, or if these signs were too subtle, then by the crest emblem, a dogfish, tattooed on her back.

In this condition, she was found by a young man on a beach in Skidegate Inlet. He brought her aboard his canoe and took her to the house of his parents, where she was bathed and fed, while her hosts and their other guests waited to hear her tale.

"My family owned a hat in the shape of a

double cormorant," she began at last. "It was a powerful hat. When a dancer wore it, the earth quivered under his feet, and he could dance for days. My elder brother was extremely fond of this hat, and though my father had told him never to put it on without ceremonial preparation, and never to wear it except when ritual required, one day my brother wore it out fishing. When he came home from that trip, he wore it no longer, and though he had left with three friends, he returned alone.

"He told us the hat had kept falling off while he was fishing, and that finally in anger he had thrown it into the water, saying, 'There! It won't stay on my head. Try it on yours!'

"He said they caught trout, and that evening they cooked them and laid them on skunk cabbage leaves. And a copper-colored frog hopped out of the bushes next to their campsite and lit on my brother's fish. He threw the frog back into the bushes, threw away the fish and cooked another, but again the frog appeared and landed on his fish. My brother threw the frog back into the bushes again, and cooked another fish. When the frog reappeared once more and landed on that fish too, my brother threw fish, frog and all into the fire and piled on fresh wood and fanned up the blaze.

"He said the frog sat in the flames for a long time, glowing like a coal, and then suddenly exploded and put out the fire. And all that night, as he and his friends tried to sleep, he said they heard a woman's voice crying, saying something about her child.

"When they set out for home the next

morning, they passed a woman standing on the shore. She had a hummingbird in her hair, and a walking stick covered with frogs, and she was crying, 'Where is my child? What have you done with my child? Where are his clothes?'

"They were too frightened to stop, but when they paddled on, they passed a man on the shore whose face was painted red and black, and he said to them, 'You will die. The first of you will die when you pass the first point, the second at the second point, the third at the third point. The prince will reach the village, and he will die when he has told his tale.'

"My brother said the first of his friends died as the man had said, and the second and the third. My brother himself was the one who returned alone to the village, and when he had told us what I have told you, he also died. He was sitting in front of us talking, just as I sit now in front of you, and then he was dead and could tell us no more."

Here the young woman paused, and for a moment there was no sound in the house except the low sound of the fire. She stretched her fingers, watching her hands as if it surprised her to see them still move; then she put them back in her lap and continued.

"Soon after that, a strange woman came to our village. A red hummingbird perched in her hair, and when anyone spoke to her, she seemed not to hear them. She said only one thing, over and over. 'Where is my child?' she said, 'and where are his clothes?'

"The old ones told us there would be more trouble, and there was. My grandmother made me hide in the latrine. I objected, but she insisted. A few days later, while I was still hiding, I felt the earth shake. Then a huge fire was burning all over the village. Even the sea and the sky seemed to burn. When I came out, no one else was alive, and nothing was left. The canoes, the houses, the storage boxes, the poles were all smouldering ashes.

"I saved only one thing—a small stone bowl which my grandmother gave me when she made me hide. With that under my arm, I started walking, and I had walked many days when I came to this inlet last night. Your son, as you know, found me on the beach this morning."

In the silence that followed, she saw the old slave woman who had led her to the bathing place, now whispering to the chief's wife, and the chief's wife whispering to her husband. Another slave brought the girl more food.

"My wife and I have just recently lost a daughter," said the chief. "The new pole in front of the house is her mortuary pole."

"The crest on that pole," said the girl, "is one of my own crests, the dogfish."

"Then let us adopt you as our daughter, in place of the one we have lost," said the chief's wife. "The young man who found you this morning is of the same side of the Haidas as you are. He will be your new brother."

Some days later, a potlatch was held to confirm the adoption, and the story was told and retold, so that the fame of the young princess spread throughout the Islands. And as she was of marriageable age, messengers soon began to arrive at the chief's house, sent by the nephews of other chiefs, seeking his adopted daughter's hand.

Within the year, Wealthsound was married—but her husband, like the Raven's wife, came from the mainland, and to that country he and his bride returned. For many years, Wealthsound did not see her adoptive family, yet she told her children countless stories of Haida Gwaii and thought constantly of returning.

One day her youngest son came to her saying, "Mother, the other children taunt me, saying I have no grandparents or uncles. They say I am a foreigner and an orphan's child."

This insult, though it came from the mouths of children, settled Wealthsound's mind. She resolved to return, with her children, to the Islands and to rejoin the family which had adopted her many years before. Her husband, in an effort to make amends for the insult, agreed to her departure and furnished her with wealth and provisions, canoes to carry them, and slaves to paddle the canoes.

So Wealthsound arrived once again in Skidegate Inlet, dressed this time in finery, and carrying more than a little stone bowl.

Her adoptive parents were dead. The young man who years before had found her on the beach and brought her home now sat in his father's place. He welcomed her as his sister, and her eldest son as his heir.

All looked well, and might have been so. But the eldest son was too eager. He took to sleeping with his uncle's wife whenever his uncle, the chief, was out hunting, and before long news of this impertinence reached his uncle's ears.

"I am going hunting again tomorrow," said the chief, "and I will be gone for several days." Then he readied his hunting gear, and next morning he left, but he did not go far from the village. That night, he surprised his wife and nephew in bed, denouncing them both.

He placed his terrified nephew into a large wooden storage chest and closed the lid, caulking the seams with spruce gum and tying the lid down securely with cedarbark line. Then he had the chest set adrift on the falling tide.

"No one," he thought, "will ever again see this nephew of mine alive, nor will he ever again sleep with another man's wife."

The young man, hunched in his chest, bobbed and floated for many days until, starving and feverish, he realized he was floating no more. He thought he heard the sound of surf and the voices of women, but he was too weak to cry out. Then the lid of his chest was thrown open and the light of day blinded him. Yet he heard once again, distinctly this time, the voice of a woman, which seemed to be saying, "He's mine. Take him home."

When he woke, he found himself looking up at the ceiling of a handsome, six-beam house. When he stirred and sat up, he heard a warm, sharp voice saying, "Welcome, my son-in-law. Come and sit down by your wife."

A slave led him to sit by a young woman whose face he did not recognize, but whose voice when she spoke to him he knew he had heard before.

"It was you," he said, "who rescued me from the box."

"It was I," she said. "This is my father, the chief of our village," and she indicated the old man seated across the fire. Beside the chief, sharing his carved settee, was the oldest woman he had ever seen.

"And my grandmother," said the girl.

"Hello, my grandson," said the old woman. Her voice was like the sound of stones being dropped into water.

Eagle skins hung on the walls all around the house. An eagle flew in through the smokehole and landed well back from the fire, and the young man watched it carefully. It took off its skin and hung it up, then came down into the center of the house and sat with the others. When it came out of the eagle skin, it looked exactly like a human being.

"This is my son," said the chief.

"Hello, brother-in-law," said the man who had just been an eagle.

It was, as the young man soon learned, a village of eagles. His wife, his brothers-in-law, and everyone in the house had an eagle skin hanging on the wall.

"I want to go hunting with your brothers," he said that evening to his wife.

"I will ask my father," the Eagle Princess said.

Sometime later, the chief summoned him.

"Take this skin," said the chief. "I wore this one myself when I was your age. Good luck, Eagle Prince."

"Only one thing," said the old woman, who continued to sit at the chief's side. "If you hunt with the eagles, you may sometimes see the giant clam. It is stronger than you are. Don't touch it."

The young man entered the eagle skin, flew through the smokehole and tried out his wings. That very day, he caught a fine spring salmon. Before the month was out, he was helping his brothers-in-law bring in seal, sealion and killer whale.

Again the old woman warned him about the clam.

Next day, the Eagle Prince brought in a killer whale unaided. He was very pleased with himself, and once more the old woman cautioned him about the clam.

Next day he caught two killer whales. And the day after that, for the first time, he saw the clam. He circled back and flew low over it. He thought it did not look stronger than he was.

He grazed it with his talons, thinking to frighten it, but found he was stuck fast, unable to let loose. He squeezed hard, beat the air with his wings and let out his eagle cry, but the clam did not budge. It began to draw him down.

As his head was level with the waves, one of his brothers-in-law came to his aid, sinking his talons into the Eagle Prince's shoulders, and beating furiously with his wings. But the two of them together were not enough, and both were drawn down. A third, a fourth, a fifth added himself to the pillar of beating wings. All the chiefs and princes of the eagles, each with his talons in another's shoulders, were drawn into the water like a chain.

And the old woman back at the village

heard the cries and said to herself, "That is the clam and my arrogant grandson."

Taking her own eagle skin, which was thin and badly frayed, the old woman flew stiffly off. Only the shoulders and head of the last eagle in the chain were still above the water. She grasped this eagle with her talons and stroked the air with her frail-looking wings.

Slowly the tall pillar of eagles rose from the water, and as each one rose above the waves, he heard for the first time the song which the grandmother of the eagles was singing. As the last eagle reached the surface of the sea, a great cracking noise was heard and the earth shook like a leaf in the wind.

The eagles flew back to the village still linked as a chain, and with the grandmother of the eagles at the top, still quietly singing. But in the claws of the last eagle in the chain hung a limp and empty eagle skin. The Eagle Prince remained in the sea with the clam.

His wife was inconsolable. She would neither eat, nor sleep, nor fly.

Finally, the old woman spoke to the chief. "She will die," said the old woman, "unless you resuscitate her husband, disobedient though he was."

So the Eagle Chief went to a corner of his house, where he opened a stone box and uncovered the hole in the sea. Into it he reached with his dip net, sifting through everything that has ever been lost in the oceans. At length he assembled his son-in-law's bones, wiped them clean one by one and laid them out on a bed of fresh seaweed. Then he leapt over them, back and forth, for four days. On the second day, new flesh covered them. On the third, they began to move, and on the fourth day, the Eagle Prince stood before his wife once more, and before the old woman, promising never to doubt her word.

Some days later, the Eagle Prince resumed hunting, bringing in salmon, seal, sealion, porpoise and whale. But in time he grew silent, and seemed to take less pleasure in his life among the eagles.

"What ails your husband?" said the chief to his daughter one day.

"He is homesick, father," said the Eagle Princess. "He would like to return to his village in the country of the humans." She paused. "I would like to go too."

The Eagle Chief said nothing on the subject

for several days. Then he called his son-in-law to him.

"My daughter has told me of your wish to return to your own people," said the chief. "You may go. And since she wishes to go with you, my daughter may go also. But take these three pebbles. To reach your village, you must fly some distance. When you get tired, drop one of the pebbles. You will be able to rest where it falls."

They left the next morning, flying westward. One carried a pebble in each claw; the other carried a pebble and a small bundle. At evening, they dropped one of the pebbles. Where it fell into the sea, a small wooded island appeared, and they landed to rest there.

It was the same for the three days over open water. On the fourth day, when they left the island formed by their last pebble, they could see land on the horizon, and that day they arrived at the village on Skidegate Inlet. Smoke curled up from the houses which the Eagle Prince had long thought he would never see again.

They set their small bundle down on the beach and perched near the smokehole of the chief's house to hear the news. There they learned that the Eagle Prince's uncle was dead and had been succeeded by his second nephew. But the Eagle Prince also heard the voice of Wealthsound, his mother. She was still alive.

He flew to the ground, took off his eagle skin and walked through the doorway of the house of his brother the chief.

"My brother," he said, "I have returned. I have a wife with me, and our belongings are on the beach. Are we invited in?"

"You are invited, my brother," said the chief. "I had not expected to see you again, but I have thought of you often, and you are welcome."

The Eagle Prince called in his wife, and his brother's slaves were sent to the beach for the bundle which the eagles had brought with them. Small though it had been, it was now so large that many slaves were required to carry it, for it consisted of many boxes, containing the flesh of many seals, sealions and whales.

The Eagle Prince was reunited with his mother, gifts were exchanged, and Wealth-sound gave to the Eagle Princess a small stone bowl—the one she had brought with her to that village after the fire at Cumshewa Inlet.

The eagles stayed on in the chief's house,

and the Eagle Prince went out each day in his eagle skin, hunting whales and other game. He was much admired by all the women in the village, but he paid no attention to any except one, whom he began to eye constantly, and who eyed him in return.

His wife, the Eagle Princess, went to the stream each day to bathe, and dipped up water in her small stone bowl, stirring it with the eagle feather she always wore in her hair. One day, as soon as she touched it with the feather, the bowl of water turned milky. Then it grew thick and slimy as she stirred. She returned to the house and unpacked her eagle skin. Just as she was putting it on, her husband returned.

"Where are you going?" he asked, but she would not speak to him.

She flew through the smokehole without a word. The Eagle Prince put on his own skin at once and flew after her, calling.

"Don't follow me," his wife cried. "Go back to the other woman."

But he kept on following, calling to his wife, until she wheeled suddenly, high over the open sea, and stared at him, singing a song he had never heard.

His feathers withered like leaves. And in his ears as he fell was a sound like the croaking of frogs.

Epilogue: The Dogfish Woman

And so we come at last to what may be the strangest and most powerful image in this little book: the image of the Dogfish Woman.

Perhaps before meeting her, you should know something about the dogfish, which in real life is a small shark, four or five feet long, frequently seen on the Northwest Coast. This diminutive shark was extremely important in the crest iconography of the Haidas, and perhaps we can judge just how important it was by the fact that the larger sharks—which are also quite plentiful—are called in the Haida

language "dogfish mothers." The dogfish itself, by contrast, is never called the child of the shark.

What's more, the classical representation of the Dogfish may well be the most ingenious exercise in abstraction in the whole Haida bestiary. Though at first it might seem impossible to relate the broad face, the great staring eyes and long forehead of the traditional Dogfish crest to the narrow-bodied, sleek little shark of the same name, every step in the transition is logically and carefully thought out, and all the important anatomical features of the fish are captured in the symbolic form.

That elusive and compelling creature, the Dogfish Woman, is generally shown with most of the identifying characteristics of the Dogfish crest itself—a high forehead with deep wrinkles, gill slits in the cheeks, sharp triangular teeth and unnerving elliptical pupils. In addition, she has some anatomical oddities of her own. Her nose has become a beak which curves into her mouth, and her lower lip carries the labret worn by aristocratic Haida women.

We should tell you, then, the story of her relationship with the dogfish, and how she came to look as she does. But we can't—for this myth, which must have been one of the most important in the oral literature of the Haidas, is lost. For this book at least, the Dogfish Woman has become the symbol of the countless stories which have been lost from the once vast store of Haida myth and poetry. We have only a few hints of her story, and the principal one is her reputation as a shaman of extraordinary attainments, whose power derived from the spirit of the dogfish, who was her familiar.

Perhaps somewhere some old person re-members a little more of the story, or perhaps in some forgotten archive some note by a long-gone anthropologist will tell us more. For now, we must let her grey image close the door through which we have glimpsed the ghosts, half-remembered, half-invented, of a few of the beasts, monsters and improbable people who lived and relived their fantastic adventures in the imaginations of the old Haidas, constantly renewed and recreated in the old days by the genius of their poets, sculptors, painters, danc-ers and singers.

The colorful pageantry that resulted from all that energy is now not even a memory, but merely something we try to reconstruct from fragments of song, from time-dimmed, immobile images frozen in museum attitudes, and from scanty accounts by ignorant outsiders.

The light the Raven stole has grown a little dimmer for all of us, but it still flickers faintly in the houses of the people of Haida Gwaii. And the old magic of the Islands, which were there even before mythtime, is still strong. The old ghosts will continue to haunt the land until new spirits can be born.

This may be another time before anything was.

But on the banks of some river somewhere, you may be sure, someone or something, even if it isn't us, is living, and the Raven and the Mouse Woman are wily enough to keep their stories going.

About the Authors and the Artist

Bill Reid is one of the most widely respected Native American artists living today. He is also the author of *Out of the Silence* and *Indian Art of the Northwest Coast: A Dialogue on Craftsmanship and Aesthetics* (with Bill Holm).

Robert Bringhurst is an internationally respected poet and student of Native American languages and culture. He is the author of a dozen books of poetry, including *The Beauty of the Weapons; Pieces of Map, Pieces of Music;* and *The Calling: Selected Poems 1970–1995.* He is also the author of *The Black Canoe: Bill Reid and the Spirit of Haida Gwaii* and (in collaboration with Catharine McClellan) *Part of the Land, Part of the Water: A History of the Yukon Indians.*

Library of Congress Cataloging-in-Publication Data

Reid, William, 1920–

    The raven steals the light: Native American tales/
Bill Reid and Robert Bringhurst; illustrated by Bill Reid.

       p.   cm.—(Shambhala centaur editions)

    ISBN 1-57062-173-X (alk. paper)

    1. Haida Indians—Folklore.   2. Tales—British
Columbia—Queen Charlotte Islands.

I. Bringhurst, Robert. II. Title. III. Series

E99.H2R45   1996   95-30968

398.2′089972—dc20   CIP